Managing Priorities and Deadlines

28 Secrets to Time Management Success

Managing Priorities and Deadlines

28 Secrets to Time Management Success

by **Marcia Dennis**

SkillPath Publications

Editor: Bill Cowles

Layout and cover design: Jason Sprenger

ISBN: 978-1-929874-90-3

10 9 8 7   17   16   15   14

Printed in the United States of America

Table of Contents

Part Three: Your Pacing Choices

Part Four: Your Personal Choices

Introduction

Beliefs about time

- Time is the great equalizer. Whether you are young or old … a CEO or bank teller … educated or not … you have the same 24 hours a day everybody else has.
- You alone are responsible for how you spend your time.
- Time management is not about time. It's about choices.
- Your choices about how you spend your time make a difference.
- If you're not achieving what you want to achieve, it is because you are making the wrong choices.

Every choice you make is an opportunity to advance closer to your goals and dreams.

Have you really listened to yourself lately?

"I don't have the time."

"Where has the time gone?"

"If only I had more time."

"Time just got away from me."

What if you started thinking …

"I am responsible for how I spend my time."

"I can manage my time differently and get better results."

"I am in charge of my time. Nobody else is."

"I am not a victim."

You're in charge!

Discover how to begin making different, better choices in four critical areas of your life. Start rowing the boat in the direction you choose and start feeling a new sense of inner personal control and direction.

Part One:

Your Productivity Choices

Choice 1:

Start your day with a plan

The most successful people have at least one thing in common: A plan for where they want to go. Experts say people who spend 15 minutes planning their workday can free up as much as an hour of bonus time each day. Planning takes time at the beginning. But it will save time in the end.

The most important thing about a plan? Simply having one. By staying on task and working toward your goals, your day will be more directed than if you "wing it." A plan is motivating. And it reminds you that you are in charge.

✓ Self-Check:

How do your planning skills rate?

I do my planning at the same time every day.	Yes	No
I do not fill my day with back-to-back activities.	Yes	No
I sometimes block off time for working alone on tasks that are important to me.	Yes	No
I believe balance is important. I leave time for work and family.	Yes	No

Do you see some room for improvement?

Action Plan:

Set a planning time for each day and stick to it for a month.

Leave open times throughout your day to adjust your plan as needed.

At the end of one month, look back to see what worked well and what can be improved.

Tips for making a plan that sticks:

- Your plan doesn't have to be fancy. Jotting down thoughts on a pad is fine.
- Make a daily appointment with yourself to plan, either when you awake in the morning or the night before.
- Be realistic about how much you really can accomplish in one day.
- Think about your priorities and how you will achieve them.
- Schedule loosely so you have time to deal with the unexpected.

It's your choice:

Start each day clear and confident about what you want to accomplish.

Choice 2:
Make a list and check it off

A to-do list is one of the most amazing inventions of modern times. When you have too much to do and feel completely overwhelmed, it can instantly put you back in the driver's seat. The simple practice of keeping to-do lists often is a major leap forward for people striving to get control of their time. First, you have a list of everything you need to do all in one place so you won't forget things. Second, when you prioritize the items, you have an at-a-glance plan for tackling what's important first.

To-do lists can:

1. Keep you from feeling out of control

2. Guide you through decision making

3. Help you prioritize

4. Jog your memory

5. Provide an insightful overview of your day

6. Make your life easier

7. Motivate you

8. Reduce stress

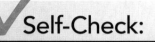

Self-Check:

Are you maximizing your use of to-do lists?

I've made list writing a habit. I do it every day, throughout the day.   Yes   No

I write detailed lists. I put down exactly what I plan to do and when.   Yes   No

I put the most important things to do at the top and the least important at the bottom.   Yes   No

I break projects or tasks into steps.   Yes   No

I remove items only if they are completed.   Yes   No

I don't allow lists to force me to do things that are no longer important. I keep revaluating my lists.   Yes   No

I cross off what I have accomplished—it feels great!   Yes   No

Action Plan:

Make a separate list of the steps you marked "no."

Put these steps into action for the next month.

At the end of one month, retake the Self-Check and repeat the plan as needed.

It's your choice:

Write to-do lists throughout the day and transform chaos and confusion into control.

Choice 3:
Order your goals according to importance

Time management is not about speed. It's about priorities. If you want to make good use of your time and feel satisfied at the end of the day, you must focus on accomplishing what is important to you. According to organizational expert Julie Morgenstern, author of *Organizing From the Inside Out*, many people think "I'll do the things I have to first, then the things I want to." The only problem is, there's never any time for the things you want to do.

Remember: All the items on your to-do list are not equally important. The 80/20 rule applies to time management as well.

✓ **Self-Check:**

Of these nine goal-setting areas of your life, circle which ones are your highest priorities now:

1. Personal	6. Recreation
2. Professional	7. Community
3. Family	8. Relationships
4. Financial	9. Spiritual
5. Health	

Action Plan:

Rank in order the importance of the goal areas you circled by answering these questions about each one:

Why am I doing this?

What happens if I choose not to?

Will it matter five years from now?

Will it contribute directly to my goals?

Will it impact the bottom line?

Now, look at the goal areas you didn't circle the first time through. Have you changed your mind about any of them?

It's your choice:

Spend your valuable time on what's important.

Choice 4:
Put deadlines on tasks, projects, goals

You have a big task hanging over your head with no real deadlines. Every day you don't make progress, the pressure builds. Give yourself a kick in the pants: Set a deadline. It can have an almost magical effect on your motivation. Goals without deadlines are eliminated, put off or never started at all. Deadlines will get you focused, help you organize your thoughts and ideas and stimulate action. As you get closer to a deadline, you may even become driven to meet it. Worst case, you miss the date. No big deal. You're further along than you would have been. Learn from it, set a new deadline and move on.

Parkinson's Law: "Work expands so as to fill the time available for its completion."

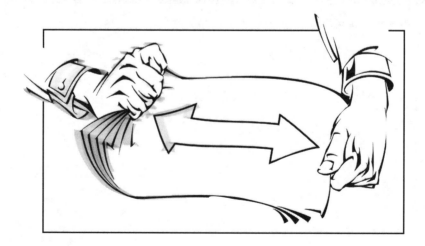

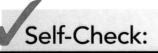 # Self-Check:

Ask yourself: Do deadlines …

Motivate me?	Yes	No
Intimidate me?	Yes	No
Challenge me?	Yes	No
Restrict me?	Yes	No

Other: _____

_____

_____

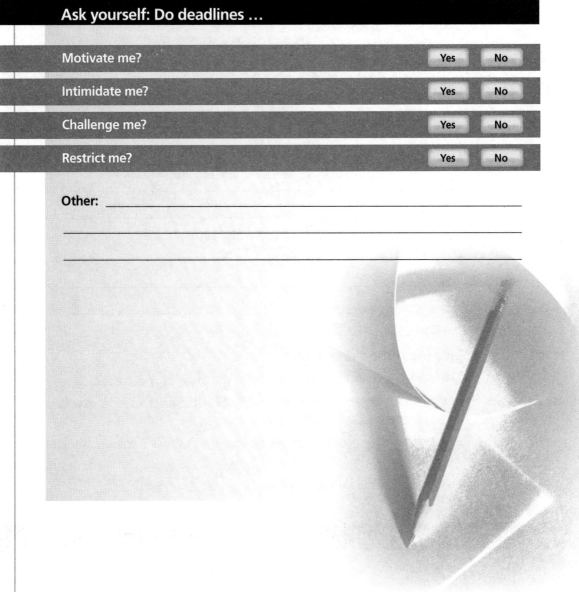

Action Plan:

Think of a project or task you just can't seem to get going on. Break it down into subtasks with three deadlines:

Deadline #1 _____

_____

_____

Deadline #2 _____

_____

_____

Deadline #3 _____

_____

_____

Tips for setting deadlines:

- Set a realistic deadline, one that causes you to stretch, not break.
- Make a public commitment to the date. Sign a contract, or agree to present part of your project at a meeting.
- Do something right now toward meeting the deadline. Eventually, you'll reach the finish line.

Now watch how quickly you complete it!

It's your choice:

Put deadlines on your goals and eliminate the excuse "I'll do that later."

Choice 5:

Be organized, but don't obsess about it

When your work area is organized and clean, you have more time to focus on people and projects that are priorities. Agreed. However, it is possible to be too tidy for your own good. Do you have to line up your pens according to color? Alphabetize the books on your shelf? Dust the top of your desk several times a day? Do you get angry or otherwise overreact when things aren't organized according to your standards? You're only setting yourself up for frustration and stress.

In the book *A Perfect Mess: The Hidden Benefits of Disorder*, author Eric Abrahamson, Columbia University professor, says a moderate amount of neatness isn't a terrible thing. But being obsessive about organization can needlessly eat up your time and energy and leave little time for what's important.

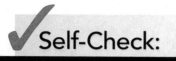 # Self-Check:

Are you too organized?

If I see a file drawer open, I have to get up and close it.	Yes	No
I can't stand for my rubber bands to be tangled.	Yes	No
If there's something on the floor, I have to stop and pick it up.	Yes	No

Think of someone you know or work with who is an organization freak. Now list all the characteristics of this person that lead to this obsession and how they cause problems in his or her work life:

_____   _____

_____   _____

_____   _____

Place a * next to those characteristics you sometimes are guilty of. When you see them manifested in your own life, think of this person and make a promise you won't suffer the same negative consequences.

Action Plan:

Make a list of the costs and benefits of over-organization.

Think of the way your behavior is distancing you from others—like your employees or colleagues.

Commit to letting go of just one "obsession" a week until they are all gone.

It's your choice:

Accept a little messiness. Your time can be better spent on other things.

Choice 6:

Drop activities that tax your time or no longer serve you well

At some point, you must come to grips with the fact that time is limited. There clearly are not enough hours in the day to do all you want to do. By eliminating less important activities, you can free up time for activities that are priorities.

Think what it would mean to your life if you stopped doing things that are not useful or necessary. If you're wasting time writing reports no one reads, attending meetings that never accomplish results or receiving reading materials from others of no value to you, stop it. Just because you've always done it that way doesn't mean you have to continue. Certain people, causes and organizations may have been important to you at one time, but aren't now.

✓ Self-Check:

Why do you keep doing activities that have no real value?

It makes me feel important.	Yes	No
I'm afraid to say no.	Yes	No
I never really think about it.	Yes	No
I would feel guilty if I stopped.	Yes	No
I feel better about myself.	Yes	No

Action Plan:

For one week, keep a diary of activities and routines you do out of habit that do not have to be done any more:

Which activities can be cut back?

Which can be postponed?

Which can be dropped?

It's your choice:

Have the courage to challenge and eliminate activities that you do on autopilot.

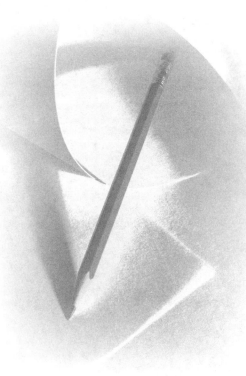

Choice 7:
Consider waiting time a gift

Oh, if you only had an extra hour every day. You could get so much done in those stolen moments. Well, the truth is that most people can carve out hours a day, simply by identifying and using hidden waiting time to their advantage.

When was the last time you had to wait in a conference room, wait for a meeting to start or wait in a client's lobby? Sometimes precious moments of time are dropped into your lap. Take advantage of them. Wherever you are, it is a good time to refocus, organize the rest of the day and make lists.

The secret is to plan ahead: Bring work with you wherever you go so you don't have to waste your time reading old magazines or sitting and doing nothing.

✓ Self-Check:

Do you see where you have valuable waiting time?

Today I spent _____ minutes/hours waiting.

I used that time to: _____

A better use of my time would have been to: _____

_____

_____

Action Plan:

Keep your own list of things to do when you're "in between," such as:

Planning

Rethinking goals

Assigning deadlines

Making phone calls

Reorganizing your schedule for the rest of the day

Catching up on reading

Going through mail and correspondence

Taking a brisk walk

Making more lists

Relaxing

Breathing

It's your choice:

You can sit and stew when you have to wait.
Or you can look at waiting time as a gift in disguise.

Part Two:

Your People Choices

Choice 8:

Set limits on people who waste your time

It's difficult to be a good time manager and, at the same time, deal with friends in need, telemarketers just doing their jobs or people who ramble. You don't have to allow certain people—co-workers, friends, family members, strangers—to waste your time and drain your energy. You may be reluctant to draw the line because you fear it may hurt your relationship. But the truth is, most people will respect you for it.

✔ Self-Check:

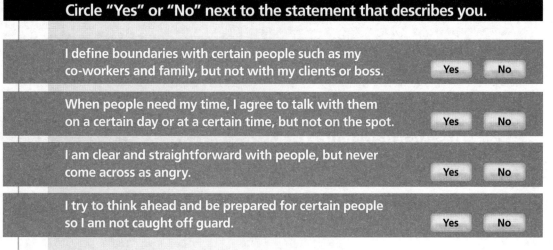

Circle "Yes" or "No" next to the statement that describes you.

I define boundaries with certain people such as my co-workers and family, but not with my clients or boss.	Yes	No
When people need my time, I agree to talk with them on a certain day or at a certain time, but not on the spot.	Yes	No
I am clear and straightforward with people, but never come across as angry.	Yes	No
I try to think ahead and be prepared for certain people so I am not caught off guard.	Yes	No

Did you mark "yes" on all four? If not, keep reading …

Action Plan:

Get the time wasters out of your office. Here are nine things you could do to discourage someone from wasting your time. Rate each of them honestly, then try the "A" strategies first:

A = I can do that   B = I can but probably won't   C = This would not work

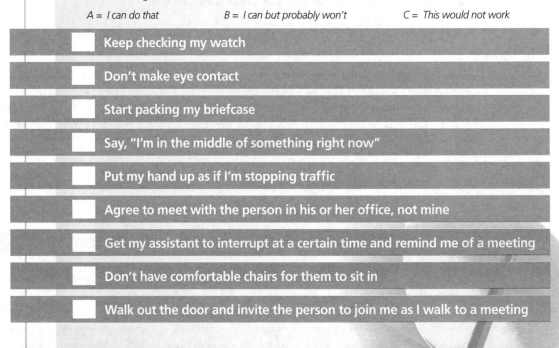

	Keep checking my watch
	Don't make eye contact
	Start packing my briefcase
	Say, "I'm in the middle of something right now"
	Put my hand up as if I'm stopping traffic
	Agree to meet with the person in his or her office, not mine
	Get my assistant to interrupt at a certain time and remind me of a meeting
	Don't have comfortable chairs for them to sit in
	Walk out the door and invite the person to join me as I walk to a meeting

It's your choice:

Draw the line with people who waste your time—it's your right.

Choice 9:

When you can't say no, say "Yes, but ..."

How many times have you automatically said yes to a new assignment, task or responsibility, only to regret it almost immediately? You cannot protect your time unless you know how to decline requests. Saying yes to everyone results in you working on their priorities and not your own. Not only that, people keep asking you to do things because you always say yes. Granted, "no" is one of the most important words in your time management vocabulary. But, let's face it, it's difficult to say sometimes. In some situations, it may be better to give a qualified "yes." Not only will you protect your priorities, but others will understand your time is precious.

✓ Self-Check:

Do any of these describe you?

Does a desire to please keep you from saying no?	Yes No
Do you ever give wishy-washy statements like "I'll try to help" rather than firmly declining?	Yes No
Do you sometimes feel bad when you can't help out?	Yes No
Are there certain people who intimidate you?	Yes No
Have you ever said yes and then wondered *Why am I doing this?*	Yes No
Have you ever said no to someone but given in when they pressured you?	Yes No
Are there certain people who make continual requests of you because you're "easy"?	Yes No

Action Plan:

When you feel you shouldn't say yes, yet can't say no, try saying:

> "Yes, I'll do it if no one else steps forward."

> "You can count on me as your Plan B."

> "Give me a call next week if you haven't worked it out."

> "I'll think about it and get back with you."

> "I really don't have time to do a good job. It wouldn't be right for me to take it on."

The 72-Hour Solution

Over the next three days, be conscious of how many times you agree to do things you don't want to do. Use the chart below to list the people you said yes to and how many times. Do you see a pattern?

Day 1: Number of times _____ People _____

Day 2: Number of times _____ People _____

Day 3: Number of times _____ People _____

Keep doing this exercise until the number of times is "0."

It's your choice:

You can keep saying yes to everyone else's priorities. Or you can start setting limits and focusing on your own.

Choice 10:

Deal with interruptions, then quickly refocus

Have you ever really thought about how many times you are interrupted in a day? Studies show 6 – 7 interruptions every hour. That's a lot. When you figure it takes 4 – 5 minutes to get back on track each time, you're talking about a potentially major time killer. Unless you work in a bubble, you will not be able to completely eliminate every interruption. But you can change how you react to them. If you spend less time getting frustrated and more time accepting the interruption and promptly getting back to the task at hand as soon as you can, your day will be less of a battle.

"Life is 10% of what happens to you and 90% of how you respond."
—Lou Holtz

Self-Check:

Identify the types of interruptions in your life:

Interruptions that come to you—like ringing phones and drop-in visitors

Other: _____

_____

_____

_____

Interruptions that you initiate—such as surfing the Web and going to get a cup of coffee

Other: _____

_____

_____

_____

Interruptions that are internal—including daydreaming and worrying

Other: _____

_____

_____

_____

✓ **Self-Check** (continued):

Does your behavior need changing?

I deal with interruptions the minute they occur.	Yes	No
I never close my door or put up a "do not disturb" sign.	Yes	No
My desk is turned toward the door and often people catch my eye and walk in.	Yes	No
I never send my phone calls to voice mail if I am at my desk.	Yes	No
When people ask if I have a minute, I always say sure.	Yes	No
Colleagues sometimes walk in with questions about projects.	Yes	No
Sometimes, after an interruption, I take a break rather than refocusing on what I was working on.	Yes	No

Action Plan:

Be aware of the role of interruptions in your life:

Keep a log of interruptions.

Write down who interrupted you and why.

Note how long the interruption lasted.

Observe how long it took for you to get your focus back.

It's your choice:

Allow time for interruptions and unplanned emergencies
and get back on track as quickly as possible.

Choice 11:
Be less accessible

Cell phones. E-mail. Pagers. Instant messages. Call forwarding. BlackBerries. In the old days, accessibility was all about being at your desk from nine to five. Today, with all the technological advances, it's about being available 24/7.

But instant availability doesn't necessarily make you more productive. Knowing when to unplug, shut it off or ignore technology is one of the key lessons in time management.

✓ Self-Check:

Are you leashed—or liberated—by technology?

	Yes	No
Do you equate accessibility with importance?	Yes	No
Do you check your e-mail each time you get a new one?	Yes	No
Do you fear turning off your BlackBerry?	Yes	No
Have you ever panicked because you left your cell phone at home?	Yes	No
Do people from work ever call you on weekends or late at night?	Yes	No
Do you check your e-mail and voice mail while on vacation?	Yes	No

Action Plan:

Dare to disconnect. Make a promise:

I will answer my phone if I want but not out of obligation.

I will keep phone calls short.

I will turn off my cell phone when I don't want to be interrupted.

I will work at least an hour before re-checking e-mail.

I will turn off the sound that notifies me when new mail comes in.

I will let voice mail take messages when I am busy.

I will check my e-mail at only certain times of the day.

I will establish clear boundaries between work and home.

I will turn off Instant Messenger.

I will not be on call 24/7. I won't expect others to be either.

I will screen calls using caller ID.

I will not give out my cell phone number.

It's your choice:

Be served—not ruled—by the technology in your life.

Choice 12:
Take responsibility— don't blame others

Being a good time manager means making good choices about your time. Unfortunately, some people would rather blame their lack of productivity and unrealized dreams on others: Their boss, spouse, customers—even the dog. But the truth is, poor time management is largely a self-inflicted problem.

Certain attitudes and behaviors that distract you from doing what matters most can be costly. Your productivity drops and so does your self-esteem.

Examples of common self-inflicted time robbers:

- Personal disorganization
- Not listening
- Indecisiveness
- Socializing too much
- Failure to delegate
- Perfectionism
- Lack of planning
- Continually taking on too much

Examples of time robbers inflicted upon you:

- Waiting for answers
- Bureaucracy
- Others' mistakes
- Traveling
- No authority
- Disorganized boss
- Changing priorities
- Unnecessary meetings

✓ Self-Check:

Identify the three time robbers that cause you the most problems.

1. _____

_____

_____

_____

2. _____

_____

_____

_____

3. _____

_____

_____

_____

Action Plan:

Rank each of the three time robbers as either "S" for self-inflicted or "O" for inflicted upon you by others.

List three things you can do to eliminate self-inflicted time robbers.

1. _____

2. _____

3. _____

List three things you can do to minimize or eliminate time robbers inflicted by others.

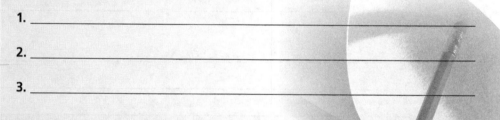

1. _____

2. _____

3. _____

It's your choice:

Be aware of the ways you cause your own time management problems and be willing to take responsibility.

Choice 13:

Avoid meetings, improve the ones you must attend

It's probably no surprise to you—one of the biggest time wasters in today's workplace is meetings. Raise your hand if non-stop meetings have ever wrecked your day and left you feeling drained and frustrated.

Studies show the average professional spends 35 – 55% of the day sitting around tables. How many times have you heard others complain "That meeting was a waste of time"? Yet unproductive meetings still go on and on. Insist that meetings be worthwhile and productive. Others will thank you for it.

✔ Self-Check:

Can this meeting be avoided?

Is there a plan for the meeting?	Yes	No
Are the objectives clear?	Yes	No
Is there an agenda?	Yes	No
Is there a capable leader?	Yes	No
Have you received background information so you know what's expected of you?	Yes	No

If you answered "no" to any of the above, this may be a meeting to skip.

Action Plan:

Protect your time investment—plan, prepare, manage and follow up:

Decide if the meeting is necessary. Could you accomplish the same thing by conference call? Voice mail? Memo?

If you're not convinced a meeting is necessary, get a second opinion.

Invite the minimum number of people needed. The optimum number of people for problem solving is 4 – 7. More than 12, forget it.

Require each person to bring two ideas to contribute. This will help avoid wheel spinning.

Create and distribute an agenda. Use questions instead of items. Questions will generate a response.

Get rid of chairs. Stand up or walk. These types of meetings will be shorter.

Begin the meeting promptly. You'll send the message you mean business.

Don't digress. Follow the agenda.

Immediately after the meeting, distribute minutes with action items and deadlines.

It's your choice:

Attend and hold effective meetings that produce results rather than waste your time.

Choice 14:

Prioritize people

In Stephen Covey's books *The 7 Habits of Highly Effective People* and *First Things First*, he states that "the essence of effective time and life management is to organize and execute around balanced priorities." That applies to the people with whom you work and live too. Some people are always supportive of you, and it can be positive and energizing to spend time with them when you're starting something new or facing an uphill struggle. Some other people might be consistently negative, critical, backstabbing or undermining. You may not be able to avoid them altogether, but you can plan to balance their influence on your attitude.

A positive environment in which you connect with the people who are important to you can make all the difference in the world in your productivity. You'll work better when you're not in a panic, avoiding people you don't want to see and feeling guilty because you're not spending time with the people you should.

When you have a lot going on and people need your advice and guidance, don't put them off. That will only create a backlog of people and add to your time management problems. Make time for them. Listen to their concerns. Give them what they need so they can get back to work. And you can too.

✔ Self-Check:

Who may need and deserve more time and attention than you're giving them?

Name them: _____

_____

_____

Action Plan:

How can you make the people you named a higher priority?

Respond to their requests as promptly as possible.

Listen rather than do all the talking or cut them off.

Don't act as if you're in a big hurry.

Ask if there's anything else they need.

It's your choice:

Make time for the people who are important.

Part Three:

Your Pacing Choices

Choice 15:

Choose productiveness over busyness

To be productive is one thing. But to be chronically busy is another. Constant motion is often a sign of bad planning, inadequate goal setting and poor time management. A *full calendar equals a full life*. There's something wrong with that thinking, isn't there?

There are three types of busyness. Do you know the difference?

1. **Manageable busyness** is productive and energizing. At the end of the day, you feel pleasantly tired but satisfied.

2. **Sporadic busyness** is like the flurry of activity that occurs at tax time or during crunch time at work. It's tolerable because you know it will end soon.

3. **Chronic busyness** takes over your life, feels wrong when it's happening and can ultimately affect your mental and physical health.

Do a pain inventory. How many of these consequences of chronic busyness do you ever feel?

Fatigue and the feeling that no amount of sleep is enough	Often	Sometimes	Never
No time for exercise	Often	Sometimes	Never
Eating when I get a minute at fast food restaurants	Often	Sometimes	Never
Losing track of how I feel	Often	Sometimes	Never
Ignoring the needs of others— it's all about me	Often	Sometimes	Never
Irritability	Often	Sometimes	Never
Anger	Often	Sometimes	Never
Loneliness	Often	Sometimes	Never

Why can't you slow down?

- I need to prove to my boss—and myself—I can do it
- I love the adrenalin rush
- If I slow down I will get bored
- People expect me to be busy
- Things will get out of control if I slow down
- I want to make a good impression

Other reasons: _____

_____

Action Plan:

Practice these four new possibilities for slowing down:

Stop yourself when you realize you've been in constant motion.

Keep reminding yourself of the negative consequences.

Take time for people—have lunch with a colleague or friend.

Spend some time alone every day to gain the new perspective you need to stop chronic busyness.

It's your choice:

Accept that you are a good person even if you don't keep up or get everything done.

Choice 16:

Get off to a running start in the morning

How you get started in the morning plays a big role in how much you get done that day. All too often, rather than digging into the important stuff, people fritter the time away on low-priority rituals.

Think about your first hour at work. Do you visit with staff? Go through mail? Balance your checkbook on-line? Actions like these are all forms of procrastination. What if you spent that prime time doing tasks with high payoffs instead? If you nail that first hour, you've created momentum and are off to a roaring start.

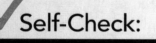

Self-Check:

What ritual do you perform every morning?

How hard would it be to replace that behavior with a more productive behavior?

_____

_____

What behavior would you replace it with? _____

_____

What might the consequences be? _____

_____

Action Plan:

How to jump-start your morning:

Leave home in peace so you don't carry over stress to your workday.

Arrive early, before there's an opportunity to get caught up in office chitchat.

Create a hit list of activities to tackle first thing. Put it in the center of your desk the night before.

Organize your work area the night before so you don't waste time looking for stuff.

Know your weaknesses. If you are tempted to spend too much time at the coffee bar, move a coffee maker into your office.

If you're in the zone, keep working—don't let anyone stop you.

Save your personal business for home.

It's your choice:

Dive into your day. No excuses!

Choice 17:
Be decisive

Do you ever go back and forth over decisions—over which conference to go to, which candidate to hire, which sandwich to order? When decisions aren't made, nothing gets done. And time is wasted. Avoidance uses up more energy than actually making the decision. When something needs to be decided or done, just do it.

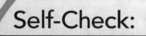 Self-Check:

Chances are, one or more of these behaviors characterizes you, and some may depend upon the situation in which you are making decisions.

I am decisive in all matters.	True	False
I don't act until I have all the information I need.	True	False
The bigger the stakes, the more decisive I am.	True	False
My colleagues see me as never wavering.	True	False
Once I make a decision I never revisit it.	True	False

Action Plan:

Caution! Do any of the following decision-making avoidance tactics sound familiar?
If so, check off and eliminate the behaviors that you recognize in your life.

Sometimes I ...

Do not think about the decision	Yes	No
Hope for the best	Yes	No
Pass the buck	Yes	No
Fail to define the problem	Yes	No
Decline responsibility	Yes	No
Set up a committee	Yes	No

It's your choice:

Life often challenges us to make decisions. Become adept
at rapidly evaluating situations and making decisions.

Choice 18:
Do one thing at a time

Hey, you there, at the computer. Are you really concentrating on getting that report done? Or are you giving directions to a colleague, responding to e-mails, answering the phone and updating your calendar at the same time? Multitasking seems like it should make you more productive. But it doesn't.

According to new research, doing several tasks simultaneously actually makes you less successful at all of them. Time management is not just about getting stuff done. It should also be about achieving some level of quality. To do that, you need to slow down and focus on doing one thing at a time.

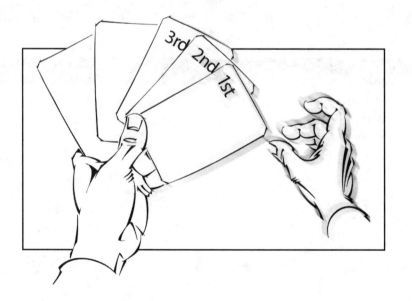

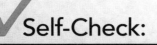 ## Self-Check:

How much multitasking do you do at work?

Way too much—I should be cloned

More and more each day

Some

Hardly any

Do you experience any of these negative consequences of multitasking?

- You make more mistakes
- You feel stressed
- You feel guilty because you aren't connecting with people
- You feel impatient with others because they are moving too slowly
- You forget more things
- Your attention span seems to be getting shorter and shorter

Action Plan:

Practice these focus exercises:

When hosting a meeting in your office, keep your focus on those in the meeting. Don't interrupt everyone else to answer the phone.

When talking on the phone, listen carefully to the other person. Don't let your attention drift to reading e-mail or shuffling paper on your desk.

When you are writing memos, reports, letters or e-mail, turn off the radio or CD player. Don't let background interference pull you away from your best work.

When working on the computer, work on one thing at a time. Don't lose your focus by bouncing back and forth among unrelated spreadsheets, databases or documents.

When you eat lunch, go to a relaxing restaurant or quiet spot in the cafeteria. Don't add stress by eating at your desk where you can also read your mail or do filing.

When driving to and from work or to visit a client, focus on being safe and arriving on time. Don't let your attention stray by talking on your cell phone.

Once you realize the rewards of these behaviors, try to extend your focus into more of your day.

It's your choice:

Try doing things one at a time and see just how much time you save.

Choice 19:

When you're stuck,
just take the next small step

That unpleasant phone call you need to make is looming like a black cloud. Every ounce of your being is resisting picking up the phone. We're talking about procrastination. If it ever gets in your way, welcome to the human race.

What is the first step in overcoming this all-too-common tendency to procrastinate? Be aware of how much your thinking has to do with it. For example, think about a project you didn't want to start. Chances are, the work wasn't all that difficult. But maybe deep down you feared you'd do a bad job because you lacked information or direction.

Did you know? **Fear is the #1 reason why people procrastinate.**

Self-Check:

Get real.

What do you procrastinate over the most? _____

_____

What keeps you from starting it? _____

_____

Check which thinking style matches your feelings:

☐ "I can start it tomorrow. That won't make any difference."

☐ "I do my best work under the pressure of a deadline."

☐ "I'll watch TV for one hour, then start."

Other: _____

_____

_____

Action Plan:

Follow the "Do's and Don'ts for Getting Unstuck":

DO ask yourself what you are avoiding.

DO put a deadline on the task to create a sense of urgency.

DO start on the worst part of a dreaded task first.

DO reward yourself after you've completed a certain task.

DON'T make the task bigger than it really is.

DON'T waste too much time struggling. Get help from a co-worker or expert.

DON'T overthink the situation. Take action instead.

It's your choice:

Take the first step on something you've been putting off.
Before long you'll look back and see how far you've gone.

Choice 20:
Think ahead and prepare

Invariably, there will be unexpected barriers to achieving your goals. A team member gets sick. Your boss changes directions. Your car gets a flat tire. Your obligations seem to grow exponentially when you get behind—just think of the last time you arrived at work a little late. Maybe you spent the rest of the day trying to gain traction. Thinking ahead can help you overcome obstacles and carry out the tasks planned.

Many time-consuming crises result from the failure to act until the matter becomes urgent. As a result, more effort is required to put the fire out. Each time a barrier gets in your way, ask yourself: What can I do to prevent this from happening again?

✓ Self-Check:

How many of these can you identify with?

	Yes	No
Failure to start early enough	Yes	No
Failure to take time to communicate	Yes	No
Failure to make sure the work you delegated was completed	Yes	No
Failure to track the progress of a project	Yes	No
Failure to have a "Plan B"	Yes	No

Action Plan:

Thinking ahead gives you a valuable head start—take advantage of it:

Are you very busy at certain times of the day? On certain days?

List ways to eliminate activities to ease the burden: _____

_____

_____

Do you ever find that unexpected blocks of time become available?

How can you be prepared to fill them? _____

_____

Will demands on your time be especially heavy during peak periods?

How can you lighten the load? _____

_____

Do you see a last-minute rush coming up?

What can you do now to head it off? _____

_____

It's your choice:

Anticipate possible obstacles to your schedule and plan how to avoid them.

Choice 21:

Know your personal prime time and ruthlessly defend it

There's a time of day when you're at your best. You're awake, refreshed, energetic and efficient. This has to do with your biological clock. Some people get up at 4:30 a.m. and hit the ground running. Others get a burst of energy mid-afternoon and are unstoppable. Still others are working away and productive in the wee hours of the morning.

Recognizing your personal high-energy zone and using that time of day to focus on the most important and demanding work is a cornerstone of time management. Do not work against your natural prime time. Lean into it and use it to your advantage.

✔ Self-Check:

Are you a morning person? Night owl?

So you're not sure when you work best? Your family and colleagues know! Ask them!

What's your most productive time of the day? _____

_____

_____

Do you need to rearrange how you work to make the most of this period?

_____

_____

Action Plan:

When your energy is low, don't push yourself. Do low-importance tasks until you're back up to speed.

Pace yourself. You can't expect to be 100% day and night.

Schedule your most important work during your personal prime time.

Don't waste your prime time watching TV or paying bills on-line. Use it for what's important.

It's your choice:

Schedule the demands of your job to fit your personal energy level. You'll get a lot more done—and a lot faster too.

Part Four:

Your Personal Choices

Choice 22:

Put "you" on your calendar

When was the last time you spent an hour devoted purely and totally to what is important to you, rather than what someone else thinks is urgent? When you forget how to make time for yourself to think, to rest, and to clear the cobwebs, your overall effectiveness will be diminished—in your work and in your life. This can leave you feeling stressed, depleted and unsatisfied. Who says "you" have to take a backseat in life?

Invest some time in replenishing yourself every day. You'll be more productive, happier and healthier—and you may even live longer.

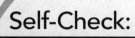 # Self-Check:

Do you have a hard time getting your work done?

Do you frequently make excuses for missing deadlines? | Yes | No

Have you missed meetings because you lost track of time? | Yes | No

Do you regularly work extra long hours and weekends just to "keep up"? | Yes | No

Do you have a hard time finding time for yourself?

Have you ever arrived home at the end of the day with nothing left to give? | Yes | No

Do you find it's virtually impossible to find time for leisure, even on the weekends? | Yes | No

Have you ever felt guilty for relaxing when there's still work to be done? | Yes | No

Have you been pushing yourself for so long, you don't even know what you would do if you did have time to relax? | Yes | No

Do you rarely take vacation time you're entitled to? | Yes | No

If you spend a lot of time thinking about how little time you have for yourself, it's time for a better plan—one that puts YOU at the top of the list.

Action Plan:

Make a promise to find time for yourself every day:

I will not spend any more time worrying about trying to find free time.

I will make some time for myself every day and put it on my calendar.

I will not spend time on unnecessary tasks and make-work chores.

I will be less busy and more productive.

I will start small. If I can find even five minutes for myself, I will take it.

Think about what you will do with your newfound time. You could …

- Take a class
- Read a book
- Invent something
- Clean out the clutter
- Meet new people

It's your choice:

You schedule time for everyone else—your boss, your customers, your doctor, your friends and family. Schedule time for yourself too.

Choice 23:

Think of self-discipline as a skill, and practice it

How many times have you started to do something you know you should do, then quit? Or not started at all? Developing the self-discipline to stick with the new time management habits you've acquired is a powerful factor in determining your success.

We've all wished we had more self-discipline—the ability to determine our conduct by judgment and principle rather than by impulse. Self-discipline—like weightlifting or tennis— must be practiced. By strengthening your ability to stop doing something you usually do, you'll build your inner power.

✓ Self-Check:

Be honest with yourself:

Do you consider yourself self-disciplined?	Yes	No

Who is the most self-disciplined person you know? _____

_____

What does that person do that makes you feel this way? _____

_____

How would that person rate your level of self-discipline? _____

_____

Which of this person's habits could you practice in your own life? _____

_____

Action Plan:

Practice these exercises daily:

If you always get a donut at morning break, give it up for the week.

Get more exercise. Instead of going home and flipping on the TV, take a walk.

Don't respond negatively to a colleague who annoys you. Try holding your tongue once. And then do it again. And again.

Don't pass along that juicy gossip you just heard. Restrain yourself.

Whenever you're supposed to be somewhere at a specific time, be there, no matter what.

Don't leave a project half-completed. Go finish it.

Keep your promises—all of them. If you say you'll do something, do it.

It's your choice:

Aim to increase your level of self-discipline by practicing daily.

Choice 24:

Ask for help

You secretly believe that you're the only one who can get the job done right, don't you? You hate asking people for help, isn't that right? You need to get over it. Some periods in your life may be more difficult to manage than others. You may be working long hours, taking work home, doing someone else's job.

It's important that you recognize and accept your limits—you can do only so much. You may be stressing and worrying about how you'll get it all done when all you need to do is ask for help.

✓ Self-Check:

Is faulty thinking keeping you from getting the help you need? Check which statements apply to you:

I feel like I have much more to do these days.	True	False
I have a strong need to be in control of things and this drives me to work harder and longer.	True	False
Sometimes I have felt like a failure when I wasn't able to get it all done.	True	False
I do not trust other people to do the work as well as I can.	True	False
I think it's easier in the end to just do the work myself.	True	False
I think asking for help is a sign of weakness.	True	False
I secretly worry someone else may do a better job than me.	True	False

Attitudes like these can be unlearned—and you can start *today*.

Action Plan:

Practice asking others to help you—here are four tips:

Ask politely. Chances are, if you're asking for help, you're already feeling tense and overburdened. Don't let these feelings spill over. Be polite: "Would you get those numbers for me by noon or let me know if that's not possible?"

Don't second-guess how the other person might respond to your request. You may think that someone's too busy, doesn't want to be bothered or isn't interested in helping you. The truth is, most people are willing to help out from time to time.

Don't delegate tasks that are trivial and needn't be done at all.

Be clear about what you need to have done, why, how and when.

It's your choice:

Accept that you are not the only one who can handle your responsibilities. Ask for help when you need it.

Choice 25:

Be perfect only when it's necessary

Of course, you want to be and do your best. And, most certainly, there is a need for perfectionism in some situations. But most things in life are pass/fail. You could put more effort in, but you won't get additional payback.

Demanding perfection of yourself all the time can be stressful. It destroys self-esteem because you never feel good enough. It hurts your chances of success because you become afraid to take on new tasks. You may also put unrealistic demands on others.

Tip: Be careful not to confuse excellence with perfection. They are not the same.

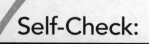

Self-Check:

Which of these factors could be underlying your perfectionistic tendencies?

Anxiety about what is expected of you	Yes	No
The need to live up to other people's standards	Yes	No
The need to live up to your own image of yourself	Yes	No
Feeling overwhelmed or paralyzed by all your tasks	Yes	No
Fear	Yes	No

Describe an area of your life in which you would like to be less of a perfectionist: _____

_____

_____

How can you edit your standards so they are more realistic? _____

_____

_____

What might happen—good or bad—if you make these changes? _____

_____

_____

Action Plan:

Learn to withdraw from perfectionism:

Say "no" to yourself when you realize you are setting unreasonable expectations of yourself.

Let go of the expectations others may have of you that have made you the way you are.

At first, choose goals that are easier to accomplish.

Don't dwell on your mistakes. Learn from them and move on.

It's your choice:

Unless your or others' safety or security demands that what you do must be absolutely perfect, strive to turn in an excellent "A-" or "B" performance and don't feel guilty about it.

Choice 26:
Finish what you start

Do you ever rush out of your office at the end of the day, leaving a desk covered with unfinished stuff? The memo you're still rewording. The flight you haven't booked. The papers you didn't file. Have you ever arrived for work the next morning and felt instantly overwhelmed by the half-done tasks lying all around? The truth is, even the most motivated people can lose enthusiasm in the middle of a project. You procrastinate and then fizzle.

If you—like many professionals today—haven't gotten the memo yet, failing to finish what you start is a big time management no-no. Not only are you having to manage everything the day brings, but you're also dealing with yesterday's baggage.

✓ Self-Check:

Consider how big a problem unfinished tasks are in your life:

Are you enthusiastic when you start a project, but lose interest about midway through? | Yes | No

Is completing a project less exciting to you than the rush of getting going? | Yes | No

Do you like a lot of variety in your life and get bored easily? | Yes | No

Is bailing out when the going gets tough a habit? | Yes | No

Look around you. Specify the projects and tasks that are unfinished and why:

For example:

I have not completed: The proposal for a computer upgrade

Why: I am waiting on pricing from a vendor

Your turn:

I have not completed: _____

_____

Why: _____

_____

_____

Action Plan:

Pick one task that is incomplete.

Specify what is keeping you from completing it.

Identify a step you can take today to further your progress.

Make a commitment to wrap up the project by a certain date.

Don't allow yourself to move on to a new task until this one is finished.

It's your choice:

Rather than feeling overwhelmed by unfinished tasks, consider completing each one a challenge.

Choice 27:

Take breaks

Working nonstop for hours at a time is not a good use of your time. Our bodies follow a cycle. We can do about 90 – 120 minutes of work before we need a break. After that, our energy decreases. Stress increases. We get tired, unfocused, downright cranky. We need a change of pace. We all work better when we take regular breaks. It's tempting to say, "I know I'm tired but I can't stop—I'll never get done." When you need a break, take a real break. The truth is, you'll be much more productive.

Think about it—it's no accident that schools build morning and afternoon recesses into their day.

Did you know that Albert Einstein, Winston Churchill, Harry Truman and John D. Rockefeller all took naps?

✓ Self-Check:

Is it time for a break?

Do you feel tired?	Yes	No
Are you having difficulty focusing? Concentrating?	Yes	No
Have you hit a block in your progress?	Yes	No
Are you checking the clock frequently?	Yes	No

Action Plan:

Try taking each of these kinds of breaks. Then see which ones left you the most refreshed. Vow to make them a regular part of your day.

Take a 15-minute nap. Okay, not at your desk. But perhaps in your car or at a park.

Close your eyes and breathe slowly and deeply.

Listen to relaxing music.

Leave your desk every day to eat lunch.

Walk around the office.

It's your choice:

Take time to get away from it all—even for a few minutes—and everyone will benefit.

Choice 28:
Think of yourself as the CEO of your time

The only behavior you can control is your own. You choose how you think about time. Feel about time. Spend time. When you realize you really do have choices when it comes to how you spend your time, you will begin to feel a new sense of control and achievement.

✓ Self-Check:

Which of the following reflect your views?
Check all that apply:

I realize I do have a choice when it comes to time.	Yes	No
I am clear about what really matters in my life.	Yes	No
I spend my time on what I value most.	Yes	No
I make relationships with others a priority.	Yes	No
I make time for myself a regular occurrence.	Yes	No
I let go of my unrealistic expectations.	Yes	No

Action Plan:

Use the space below to write a statement that summarizes your new attitude toward time management:

_____

_____

_____

_____

_____

_____

_____

_____

It's your choice:

Accept the fact that your days, weeks and future are in the best of hands—yours.